Hortus

Conclusus

Hortus

Gardens for
Private Homes

Chris van Uffelen

Conclusus

BRAUN

Contents

Preface

You don't have to die to get to paradise as long as you have a garden, according to a Persian proverb. This volume shows 53 such private paradises. Enclosed green spaces that are part of individual living, with vegetation that, like the furniture in the interior design, can be very different and directly affect the character of the open space. Ivy or cypress, bamboo or cacti – whether it looks exotic or native depends, of course, on the location. Depending on the garden owner, the private paradise can therefore be Asian, Northern or Southern European, for example. Or also Western Asian, because finally the term "paradise" comes from the Avestan term "pairidaeza", meaning "enclosure". And somewhere in this region the most prominent hortus conclusus, the biblical Garden of Eden, is said to have been located.

This "earthly paradise", counterpart to the heavenly Jerusalem, which – although described as inaccessible – was searched for centuries by theologians and geographers, but could not be found. In the middle of this earthly paradise, four rivers are said to rise and divide the garden. Obviously, because at last almost all gardens need water. And if there is just not a single river – let alone four – then it must become artificial irrigation. This technical supply, often hardly visible in the gardens of this volume, while on the other hand pools and ponds clearly show the garden design element of water. Already the gardens of ancient Persia, the oldest of all, were structured by irrigation channels, and in the upper gardens of the Villa d'Este in Tivoli, artistic irrigation certainly finds a peak in the Renaissance. This is also basically a private garden, but of course also served representation.

To represent was also a function of the ancient Persian garden and even today every private garden has a showcase function at the same time and reveals one or the other about the owner. Whereas in the past they showed grandeur and power, today gardens tend to reveal the taste and world view of the owners: Asian, North or South American planting; pool or pond or canals; sparse or lush; geometric construction or nature-like composition?

For the longest time, historic gardens were geometrical and even symmetrical, trying to tame nature. Today, even when strictly geometrically constructed, they are mostly asymmetrical. The change to this occurred in the English landscape garden, when one sought to create gardens close to nature. Most of the early and important landscape gardens were private gardens. In these private gardens, there were significantly more staffage buildings, so-called follies, than before. Staffage, a term from landscape painting, was intended to enliven the picture, to evoke moods, places or situations. Thus, even today, small buildings as part of the garden design serve their pointed statement. In addition it must be neither a Chinese tower, nor a monopteros – a tea pavilion is completely sufficient, sometimes even a peculiar fence.

Fences or plantings of the property boundaries – the outer walls of any garden – do say a lot about the garden owners. Even where they are absent, the boundary is in some way recognizable or purposefully disguised. Of course they belong to a classic hortus conclusus, otherwise it would not be conclusus, closed. From the outside, however, it does not necessarily have to appear as hermetic as Peter Zumthor's Serpentine Pavilion 2011.

On the other hand, how long would Little Briar Rose have been able to sleep without the fatally repelling thorn hedge? For despite all the aforementioned semi-public functions, the earthly paradise serves primarily as a private retreat. This doesn't always have to be about contemplation; sports and games or simply enjoying free time in an individually selected natural setting are just as good.

Landscape design: studio mk27

Location: Guarujá, Brazil
Completion: 2015
Size: 805 m^2

Jungle House

The project shows the desire of establishing a relationship between an architecture of exact lines and its surroundings.

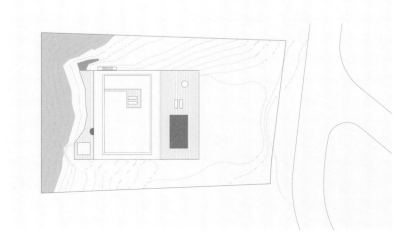

Jungle House' site plan considered a previously-existing clearing in the center of the plot, located in the midst of the Atlantic Rain Forest in Guarujá, on the coast of São Paulo. It synthetizes an investigation about how to merge modern design and tropical vegetation. The landscape design recomposed native species and the terrain organically shaped the wooden deck in the first floor. The main volume rises from the ground – apparently touching it on only two pillars – and outwards the mountains. The transversal section allows the pool to be positioned almost semi-built into the roof slab, without losing any area below it. To lower the height of the top floor volume and thereby achieve a more horizontal external proportion, the living room floor was lowered 27 centimeters relative to the outdoor deck. Due to the formal contrast and the sensorial-spatial tectonic adaptation to the environment, it seems like as if the architecture had emerged from the soil and landscape.

Landscape design: Dirtworks Landscape Architecture

Location: New York City, NY, USA
Completion: 2019
Size: 762 m^2

Rooftop Garden

The amenity spaces are defined by thoughtful furnishings as well as planter walls, crafted of custom-patinated stainless steel and select hardwoods. Key views of New York's iconic skyline as well as the Hudson River are framed within each space, creating context and interest. The terrace spaces are further defined by program elements, providing a diversity of uses within the limited area. A complete spa clad in locally sourced Onondaga Limestone complements a fully equipped kitchen and bar. A state-of-the-art audio-visual system facilitates a wide range of work and entertainment possibilities. The custom-designed dining table seats 12 for large events, and a sectional seating area with a fire table allows the family to gather in one location to enjoy this unique setting. Plantings were carefully selected to respond to the harsh climate of an urban roof condition. Sweeps of native grasses and meadow plantings provide a tempering counterpoint to the clean lines of the penthouse architecture.

The terrace celebrates
the unique urban ecology
while creating a meaningful
connection with nature.

Landscape design and architect: Alexander
Brenner Architekten

Location: Essen, Germany
Completion: 2015
Size: 3,000 m^2

Bredeney House

The Bredeney House with the attached garage separates the semi-public front garden with its generous driveway from the house garden, and forms an open garden square with the large existing trees opposite. Rhododendrons and smaller trees were placed in front of the existing trees to create a deeper image through projections, recesses and changes in height. A large, linear terrace is the stage to the open space and ends at a garden pavilion. The gentle slope extending across the area almost imperceptibly connects the different heights of the half-story offset base levels. The gentle curves of the open spaces, beds and squares contrast with the cubic, orthogonal design of the house and thus create an exciting framework for the large open center of the garden.

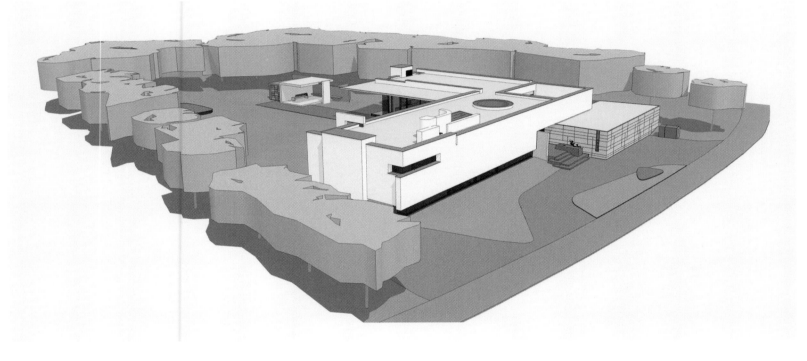

The L-shape of the house creates an exciting framework for the large open center of the garden.

Landscape design: Clemens Lutz |
Gartenarchitekt

Location: Vienna, Austria
Completion: 2015
Size: 2,800 m²

Pointe

At the end of a small street, nestled in the foothills of the Vienna Woods, a modern, elegant residential building with a clinker brick façade appears. The garden of the residence interweaves it with the forest and makes them become one. A relatively small lawn, perennials and small shrubs take on this task. Beginning as an underplanting in the forest, the planting areas partially extend to the walls where they are structured by dry stone walls, paths and erratic blocks. Due to the different climatic conditions, the sunny south-facing slope around the pool and semi-shaded areas along the edge of the forest, there are two kinds of planting: drought and heat resistant plants with a Mediterranean feel on the one hand and English Mixed Border like planting on the other. In this setting, the small lawn in front of the living room and the kitchen looks like a clearing in the forest. From the adjacent seating area, one can enjoy a wonderful view of the garden and the house, which shines in a very special light due to the surrounding semi-shade. Natural stone walls and color contrasts divide the large plot.

The garden concept allows a play of light and shadow, of transitions and mergers.

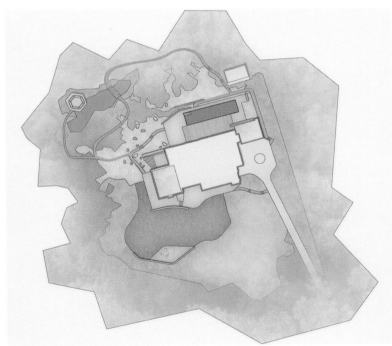

Landscape design: Eva Wagnerová

Location: Brno, Czech Republic
Completion: 2005
Size: 290 m²

Trnka Garden

A few years ago, the Trnka couple has decided to bring back life to an old house with its garden, situated in a quiet street in Brno. Nowadays, after passing through the street gate, there is a small square rest space made of stone, hidden between four cherry trees. The stone surface seems to be separated into narrow fragments, among which the water shines. Color changes are one of the basic principles of the garden. In spring there are pink buds on the bare branches until one day they completely cover the water surface. In autumn, yellow is the dominant color. This garden awakens the feeling of peace and contentment and is meant to relieve stressful life. There is no hurry after all. The garden, which was created in 2005, is far from finished, because the treetops above the water surface have not yet grown together. Moreover, the bamboo should grow to the height of the fence. For the bed of Hemerocallis, the owners are already looking for a garden sculpture that will suitably fit into the garden.

Color changes in the seasons are one of the fundamental principles of the garden.

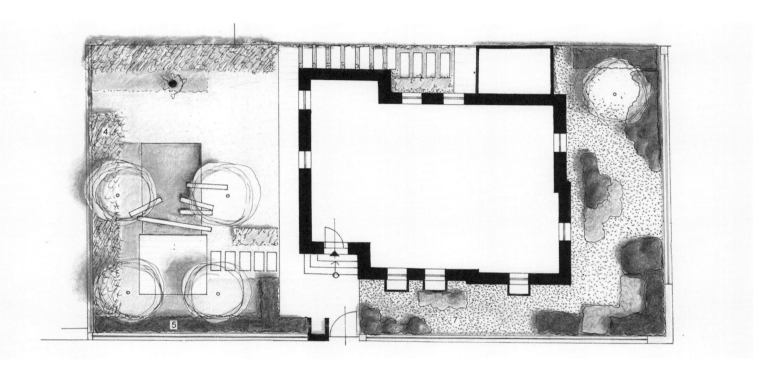

Architecture: Daniel López Salgado and Associates

Location: Oaxaca, Mexico
Completion: 2018
Size: 48 m²

Vista San Felipe

Oaxaca needs to grow vertically and the architects demonstrate how to evolve to a lifestyle that takes up less space and resources. The project is conceived in three parts. The basement and the auction occupy almost the entire area of the land and have no residential use. The body is conceived by two blocks separated by a green area to access the apartments and circulation by stairs. It is always surrounded by greenery like interior gardens and flowerpots on the entire façade of the staircase. The auction's outdoor gardens and upper terrace are also surrounded by flower boxes. The interior heights change through long transitions with changes in the level of the panels, accentuating this separation of spaces and breaking the interior monotony. A set of windows, balconies and latticework provides movement to the facades by changing from level to level. The building was conceived of integral colored concrete for a low-maintenance, clean-looking finish, as well as the way it blends with the Oaxaca City landscape, minimizing the visual impact of the volume on its surroundings.

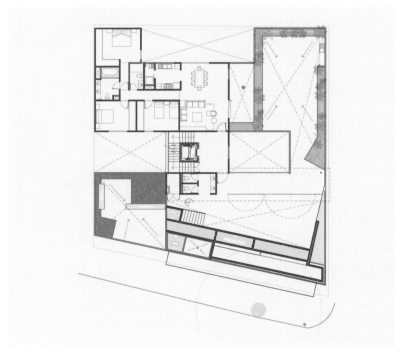

The character and identity of the project is given by the apparent ocher concrete finish, contrasting with its interior gardens which refresh the spaces.

Landscape design: Dirtworks Landscape Architecture

Location: Ocean Avenue, Sea Bright, NJ, USA
Completion: 2019
Size: 4,050 m^2

Resilient Dunescape

RESILIENT DUNESCAPE

HORTUS CONCLUSUS

The coastal community of Sea Bright suffered significant damage during Hurricane Sandy, intensifying the need for sustainable and resilient design responses. Beginning with a flat, barren site, vulnerable to flooding from the Atlantic Ocean and Shrewsbury River, this house and landscape were designed together. The house is lifted 3.7 meters above the road and placed within a new dunescape. Primary and secondary dunes were created to guide floodwaters through the landscape and provide low areas for water infiltration and storage during flood events. This hydrodynamic maneuver helped sustaining a dune ecosystem on a fragile barrier beach. Here, one trusts, is a fusion of nature and architecture: poetry in the practical.

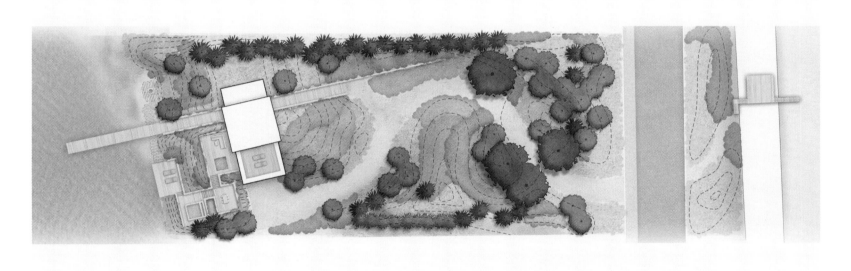

A composition of low retaining walls built into the dune provides a series of terraces for relaxing and entertaining.

Landscape design: PERALTA with MAKIA landscape architects
Architecture: PERALTA – design & consulting

Location: Wardja, Malta
Completion: 2019
Size: 10,000 m²

Rihana

New outdoor areas for everyday life are enriched by spectacular framed views of the surrounding landscape and the sea.

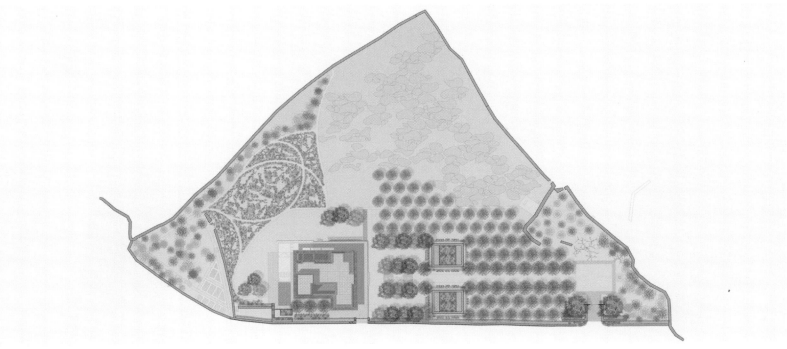

Rihana's new exterior areas of relevance, enclosed by low rubble walls were incorporated and built according to the Maltese tradition. The result was enhancing the spectacular views towards the surrounding environment and the sea. A boulevard with the juxtaposition of adult olive trees and of accurately selected drought-tolerant shrubs was created to define the perspective and reinforce a strong sense of arrival. The creation of a lawn space adjacent to the infinite pool with olive and carob trees on the edges, the design of a landscape "promenade" of curvilinear pathways cutting through a new Mediterranean garden that recalls the native landscape in the north and several secret pocket gardens with fruit and citrus trees. The building was completed with the inclusion of two horizontal planes parallel to the sea horizon line: a cantilever roof on the top and a plateau on the bottom. Together they generate new covered, usable and convivial outdoor areas for everyday life, enriched by spectacular framed views of the surrounding landscape and the sea.

Landscape design: Marmol Radziner

Location: Los Angeles, CA, USA
Completion: 2016
Size: 2,200 m^2

Mandeville Canyon Residence

Located in the Brentwood neighborhood of Los Angeles, the Mandeville Canyon Residence landscape encompasses a two-story house sited between a canyon road and a hillside in the Santa Monica Mountains. The nearly one-acre property features an array of plants, shrubs, and groundcovers that meander among the mature native sycamores. In this lush natural sanctuary that encourages outdoor living, the crisp green foliage of the plantings contrasts with the dark monochromatic backdrop of the home's dark gray brick and metal panels. Outdoor spaces coincide with the sunny locations, and plantings were designed to take advantage of these varying light conditions. Green roofs work to minimize the roof runoff, and a stormwater cistern system harvests the remaining roof and site runoff for irrigation use.

The Mandeville Canyon Residence offers beautiful plantings in a quiet and peaceful surrounding contrasting the dark bricks and metal panels of the building.

Landscape design: Fiore Landscape Design
Architecture: Assembledge+

Location: Los Angeles, CA, USA
Completion: 2019
Size: 1,670 m²

Laurel Hills Residence

Composed of three pavilions connected by a series of glass hallways, the single-story residence creates a residential oasis in the heart of Los Angeles. A walkway of concrete pavers, lined by wild grasses leads to the front door, passing a tranquil courtyard with olive trees. The entry to the house is located within a glass hallway connecting the living pavilion to the west and the sleeping pavilion to the east, establishing a sense of intimate scale before engaging with the other parts of the house. Outside, the 12-meter-long pool and ample space create a series of outdoor rooms for outdoor entertaining. A minimalist palette of charcoal-colored panels and Western Red Cedar serves as a neutral canvas, complementing the home's landscape featuring California native species. The surrounding trees and hills are taken to be the building envelope. The formal decision to build a single-story residence ensures the building is largely shaded below the surrounding tree canopy, while the deep overhang mitigates solar heat gain and shields from the sun exposure.

The entire site is treated as one is used to treating interiors: Instead of only externalizing interior spaces, exterior spaces are also internalized.

49

Landscape design: Lützow 7 Müller Wehberg
Landschaftsarchitekten

Location: Berlin, Germany
Completion: 2020
Size: confidential

At the "Kleiner Wannsee" Lake

"The Line of Beauty" establishes the dialogue of building, park landscape and lake location and offers multiple changes of perspective.

In order to honor and continue the existing in the tradition of a staged nature, a conceptual preamble in the form of shape, use, aesthetics and atmosphere was realized. A curved path creates the dialogue of building, park landscape and lake location and supplies the viewer with multiple changes of perspective. Mineral islands offer many options for lingering and contemplation. Large wildflower meadows, exotic-looking trees and pointed settings of shrub-grass plantings also form a multifaceted, spatially accentuated circuit from the entrance to the lakeshore. The deliberately chosen dialogue between clear structure and formal language as well as informal garden passages and woody plantings offer exciting, views and seasonally individual garden images for the viewer. The front yard with accentuated planting and stone bench invites to linger. Due to the generously laid out lawn areas up to the lake, an exciting park landscape is created for contemplation and places for active and individual stay.

Landscape design: O2 Design

Location: Minneapolis, MN, USA
Completion: 2018
Size: 465 m²

Private Residence Roof Garden

The garden is an excellent example of creating a dialogue between abstraction and function, inside and outside, active use and reflection.

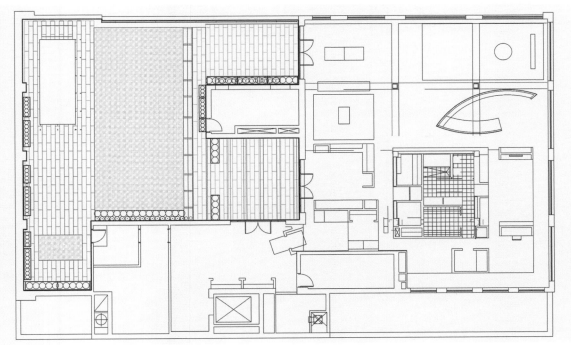

This rooftop garden atop a warehouse is located in the heart of the city and takes full advantage of the panoramic view over the Mississippi River. This project realizes the owner's desire for a modern rooftop garden and was inspired by the experimental gardens of Andre Vera and the abstract paintings of Mondrian. Using the characteristics present in both the works, the garden's vertical parapet walls became formal planes of color with perennial and annual plant materials while the horizontal ground plane became a simple neutral plane, defined with a floating rectangle of lawn and surrounding bluestone gathering areas. The architecture and garden sustain a symbiotic relationship where each is enriched by the other through managing light, shadow, form, and the ambiguity between inside and outside. The design merges art and function to create a usable rooftop garden for the desired needs of the client while making a visually and spatially provocative place to experience throughout the season.

Landscape design: Francis Landscapes - Landscape Architecture & Urban Planning

Location: Faqra, Lebanon
Completion: 2011
Size: 4,000 m²

A Magical Setting

The project succumbs to nature's legacy, with ever growing and evolving plant life and labyrinthine pathways that hide nature's well-kept secrets. Designing this garden took great discipline. The priority was to make the setting the star player. To preserve the organic feel and reflect the splendid natural surroundings, the designers had to decide when to let nature take over and when to tame it. The pathways, walkways and promenades hint at undiscovered little islands of pleasure. Even the pool house is hidden, allowing for an uncluttered field of vision, where nature and everything it has to offer can truly be enjoyed. Walking around the pool, one is taken away into mysterious walkways that tempt curiosity and guide the wanderer into groves of oak, cedar, and fruit bearing trees, making for a truly multi-sensorial, multi-seasonal experience.

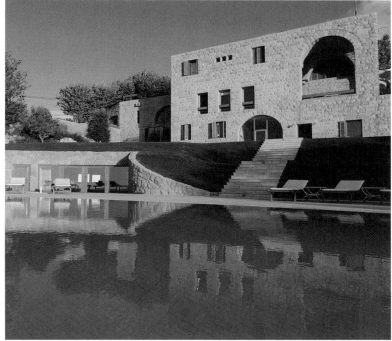

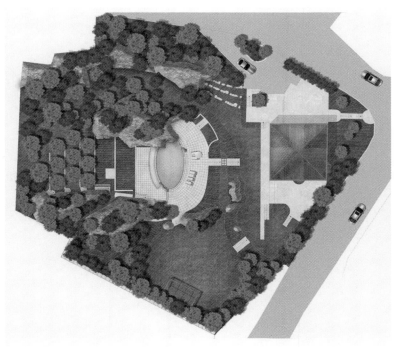

The project was designed to complement impressive existing rock formations that shape a natural amphitheater.

Landscape design: Clemens Lutz |
Gartenarchitekt

Location: Vienna, Austria
Completion: 2016
Size: 240 m^2

Doro

The roof garden extends over four terraces on two levels. The upper two terraces house, the pool and a spacious seating area surrounded by exotic plants. They are separated only by a small winter garden. The two lower terraces are in front of the dining room and the bedroom. They extend the function of these rooms. Complex technical equipment like the pool technology facilitates summer life on the terraces. Sideboards and storage spaces integrated into the wooden decks store all the necessary utensils. The majority of the plants come from the tropical and subtropical parts of the world and bring an exotic flair to the terraces. Thus, guava trees can be found next to the pink-blossoming mandevilla by the pool, aloa and New Zealand flax structure the planting around the large seating area, bougainvillea and the white capelin decorate the dining terrace. While the non-hardy plants spend the winter in the greenhouse, winter-hardy plants such as Yuccas, Sempervivum and others take over the role of structure builders in the cold season.

With one's feet dangling in the water of the pool, one sits at the level of the roof ridge from where the eyes can wander over the rooftops of Vienna's city center.

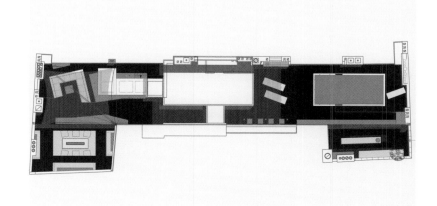

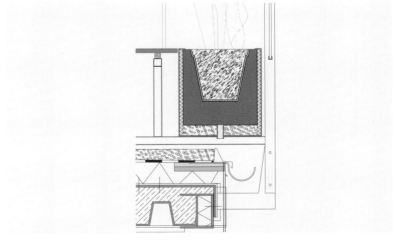

Landscape design: IPD
International Project Development
Construction: Fahrni Landschaftsarchitekten

Location: Llucmajor, Mallorca, Spain
Completion: 2015
Size: 360,000 m²

Finca Son Bí

A fountain and 12 large plant islands, enclosed by natural stone walls, were built in the garden. Each island has its own plant theme.

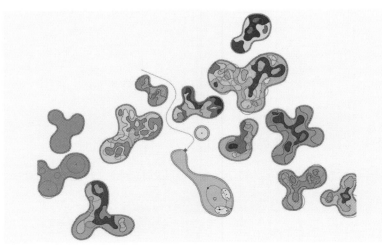

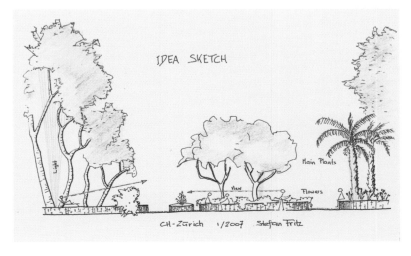

IDEA SKETCH

Light

Main Plants

View

Flowers

CH-Zürich 1/2007 Stefan Fritz

The whole island garden was underlaid with a gravel carpet, so that it can be walked through in an infinite number of variations. As a contrast to the plant islands on the gravel carpet, there is a thirteenth island. It is also elevated, but designed as a closed natural stone pavement. It begins at the edge of the island garden and meanders into the pine forest. There it can be enjoyed as a mystical place to linger. There is an attractive view through the forest into the island garden and partly to the finca's villa. At night, the scenery changes through targeted indirect lighting. So that one can use the island garden and the forest square at any time of day. In this way, exciting spatial experiences with endless mysterious vistas were created. The extensive, mostly native plant selection visibly promotes the diversity of fauna. Numerous small animal species, especially birds, insects and reptiles, have taken up the newly created habitats and continue to spread.

Landscape design: LANDLAB studio voor landscape architecture

Location: Amsterdam, The Netherlands
Completion: 2020
Size: 120 m^2

Green Oasis Amsterdam

Walls of glass with sliding doors connect the garden with the interior of the house. The design of the house and garden is inspired by Japanese architecture. In the garden this concept has been translated into a lush court with an exotic appearance. The client's main wish was a garden of stillness and the possibility to sit in many small places. Centrally located in the garden is a round pond, which reflects both the greenery and the sky and enhances the calm atmosphere. A pattern of natural stone slabs makes it possible to wander anywhere between the plants. The northside of the garden is bordered by an old high industrial wall. This characteristic raw wall has been left intact as a contrast to its sleek architecture. Several elements have been added: a long black bench to enjoy the sun for a long time and a high trellis for climbing plants. On the spot where an old door used to be, the contour is painted in Japanese-red. A second garden has been created on the roof of the sleeping pavilion. Seen from the roof terrace on the top floor the two gardens merge into a green oasis.

Within the old city center of Amsterdam a special garden is hidden behind urban façades.

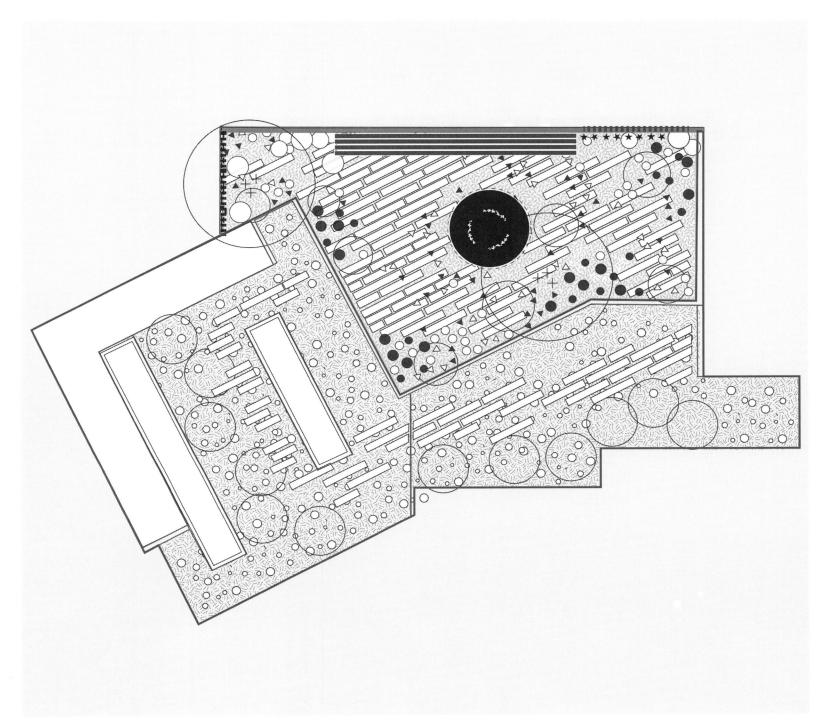

Landscape design:
SQLA Landscape Architecture Design Studio

Location: Beverly Hills, CA, USA
Completion: 2018
Size: 1,623 m²

Elden Way

The home plants with fuller foliage and texture were chosen to provide contrast with the hard edges of the hardscape.

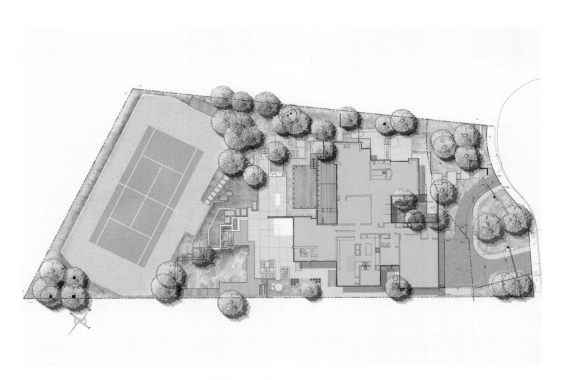

Among the first actions taken to refresh this outdoor space was incorporating corten planter walls throughout the vegetated sections of the garden space. Drought tolerate plants and native grasses such as purple fountain grass, dear grass, society garlic, kangaroo paw, and lavender were among those incorporated into this landscape remodel. Together these plants transform the garden as a whimsical private paradise. The infinity pool waterfall edge as well as the combined spa and fireplace further magnify a striking sense of serenity. Another noteworthy feature is a fully equipped outdoor kitchen and BBQ grill outlooking the residence's private tennis courts. For the tennis court area, a custom shade structure was added to shield players from the sun after a lengthy match. The last area which was remodeled was the house entry's outside corridor with a simple Zen rock garden. Doing this, a plain canvas upon which a magnificent mature oak could paint a shadow show for those entering the house was created. The Elden Way landscape remodel effortlessly proves an enchanting sanctuary for its residents.

Landscape design: Roberto Silva Landscapes

Location: Muswell Hill, London, United Kingdom
Completion: 2017
Size: 300 m²

Muswell Hill Garden

This garden is set in one of the highest points of London. It was created in a fitting way to the modern interiors of the clients. Over the balustrade planted with wisterias and pots of herbs as well as over steps cascading raised beds that reach the end of the garden, one can enter the lower level. It contains a paving of black slate contracting with the white raised beds and slate coping. Furthermore, it offers space for an included wine cellar and storage space. The second area includes the lawn sloping down to the third area as well as a decking space and different plants. An accumulation of trees forms a clear separation to the third area which was made with self-binding gravel aiming to create a jungle-like, exotic space. A fireplace and a garden-gym make this part of the garden further special. In the evening LED lighting lets the garden appear as a magical space.

The Muswell Hill contains several levels connected with steps and a balustrade while composing a contrast of dark and light throughout the garden.

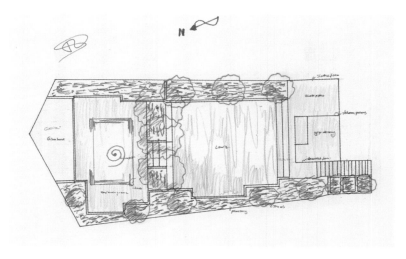

Landscape design: DS Architecture

Location: Assos, Canakkale, Turkey
Completion: 2002
Size: 3,000 m^2

Erol House

This garden is composed of ornamental squash, sunflower, lavender, pebble, cactus and clover along with a 20-meter-long temple-like structure. This structure is perceived as a separate background in different perspectives that tries to cope with the existing structure while protects again existing trees of the garden area. As an open space it connects the upper garden to the lower one. The upper garden is placed vertical to this temple-like canopy and is a whole playful, colorful and experimental space. The cabin under an almond tree at the end of this new garden is just a raised room. From here the visitor is able to view the garden he just visited. It raises him above the project lines, above the struggle of couchgrass, clover, daisy and poppy. Here is the place to enjoy the evolving visual feast. And even a better way has been found to get along with the garden moles.

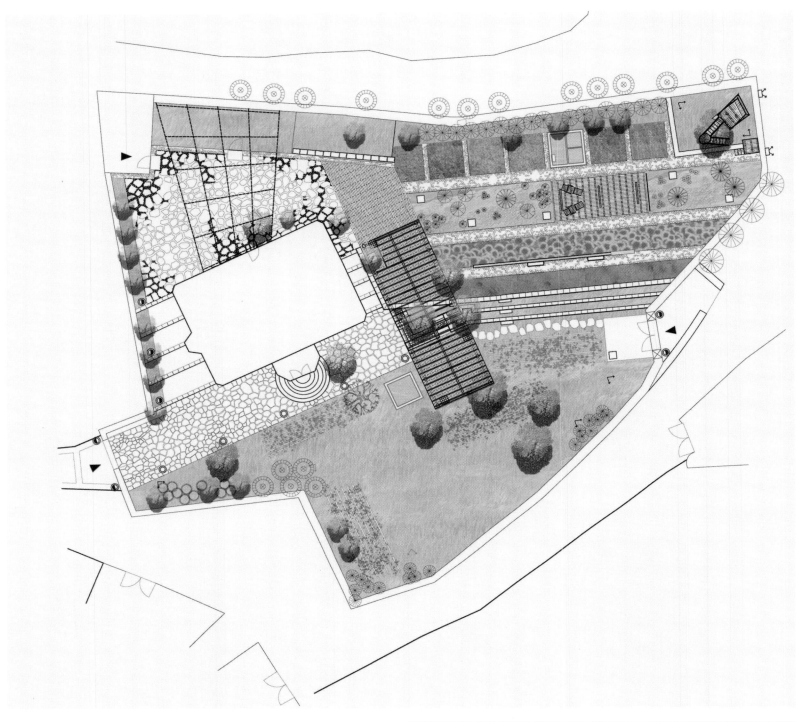

The garden was set free from
the project lines and achieved
a character through improvised
additions.

EROL HOUSE

HORTUS CONCLUSUS

Landscape design: Kräftner
Landschaftsarchitektur

Location: Mödling, Austria
Completion: 2016
Size: 145 m²

Dream Garden in Old Stock

After the renovation of a residential house in the old building ensemble, the house including 145 square meters of garden area was purchased by a young family. The special feature of the garden are the walls surrounding it on all sides to protect the garden from wind and to create an intimate, cozy atmosphere. The garden was completely redesigned: A paved terrace was created in front of the living room, and a dry stone wall made of gneiss catches the drop in height to the lawn. In the rear part of the garden a wooden garden shed was built. It provides space for bicycles, garden furniture and waste bins. The terrace is the focal point of the garden and provides ample space for a large dining table and planters. The playful flooring in light, friendly colors – quarry slabs of granite – harmonizes very well with the white painted walls. The dry stone wall made of brownish gneiss quarry stone and the corten steel beds are contrasting elements in the garden, together with the planting they frame the terrace area.

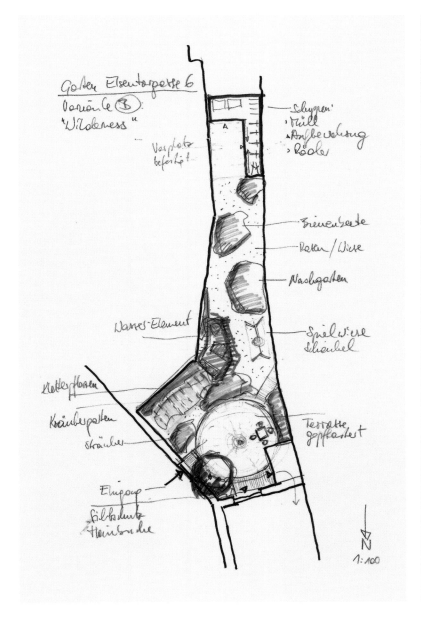

In the garden, the terrace, the lawn, the hut and the walls create a cozy and homely atmosphere.

Landscape design: Idea Verde, Atelier für Gar-
ten- und Landschaftsarchitektur

Location: Central Switzerland
Completion: 2018
Size: 453 m²

Terrace Garden

The stone figure welcomes the visitor in a friendly way and points to the drinking and washing fountain with bamboo cane inlet as a call to cleanse away the stress of everyday life.

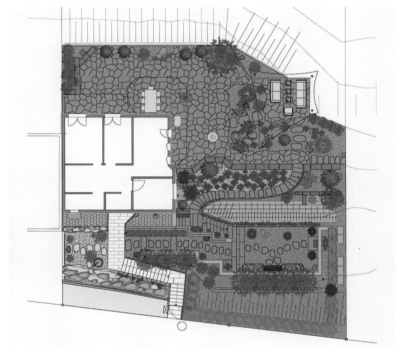

Embedded in the existing environment on the southern slope above Lake Lucerne lies this gem with a fantastic view. Many a resort would be envious of this location. Over a period of about 20 years in total, the landscape architects planned this environment on behalf of the client and executed it in several stages, adapting it to new needs. Thanks to a cooperative partnership, the now visible, very personal ambience was created in a composition of Asian and Mediterranean design elements. Giardino Secreto, meditation, as well as thoughts of Feng-Shui and Tao philosophy were integrated and implemented in the concept. The desired privacy with protection from unwanted views has been optimally achieved thanks to the choice and locations of the planting. A fully automatic irrigation system ensures vital plants even during dry periods. However, the garden presents itself as a treasure not only during the day. Also during the darkness one feels by the sensitively selected light types and locations in a discreetly illuminated paradise.

Landscape design: Charles Anderson
Landscape Architecture

Location: Denver, CA, USA
Completion: 2011
Size: 6,070 m^2

Rabbit House

The Rabbit House conveys the convergence of nature and artifice and was inspired by Denver's landscape of mountains and high desert. A significant number of existing, large trees was introduced by regionally appropriate species. Each landscape precinct displays a unique collection of mostly native plants that emphasizes the change in seasons and complements the modern architecture. A series of small and large terraces provides places to spend time outside, entertain, and observe daily and seasonal changes. An enormous sculpture, "Hare" by the late Barry Flanagan, stands in the window of the grand foyer, enticing the resident fox of the grounds. The hare and the fox, and the very different realms they inhabit, become playful symbols of the prospect and refuge provided by the bold, modern, outward-facing new residence and its adjoining, wild landscape, with its winding paths and hidden retreats.

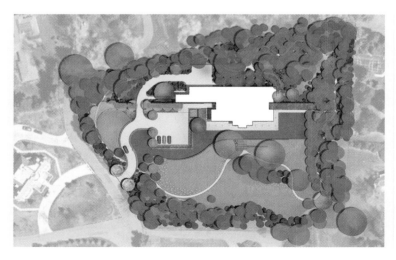

It is a landscape that is revealed not at a glance, but through a process of discovery as one wanders the paths and the meadows or observes the seasons from within the house.

Landscape design: Terragram

Location: Sydney, Australia
Completion: 2012
Size: 400 m^2

Predictable and Unexpected

The narrow courtyard to the side of the house holds a grove of tall burnt tree trunks – dead trees found on a country property, charred and scarified. The tree trunks stand in a bed of large broken slate pieces, with crushed slate under a row of black bamboo allowing for new shoots to emerge. This courtyard connects to a simple fern garden with slate and bamboo – a unifying element of the two courtyards. Here, the distinction between what is outside and what is inside is blurred. With an entire wall of the bathroom open to the garden, the only barrier being glass, as well as the gardens reflection in a wall mirror. These two narrow courtyards, consist of a number of green hills – bizarre green forms erupting out of the ground. The garden appears like a peculiar painting, framed by the windows. Its scene is like a miniature interpretation of a green mountain landscape enshrouded in clouds and mist. The hills were generated with a pyramidal polystyrene base, with hessian, growing medium, and baby tears (Helxine soleirolii) kept in place with bird netting.

The property houses many tiny courtyards. As is always the case, the smaller the space, the more attention is required to detail and intricacies.

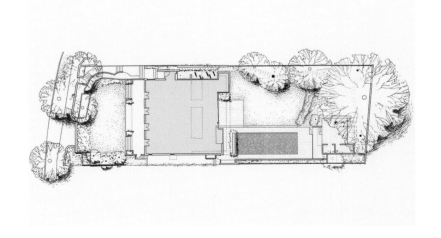

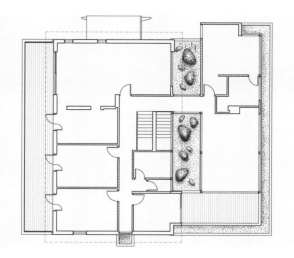

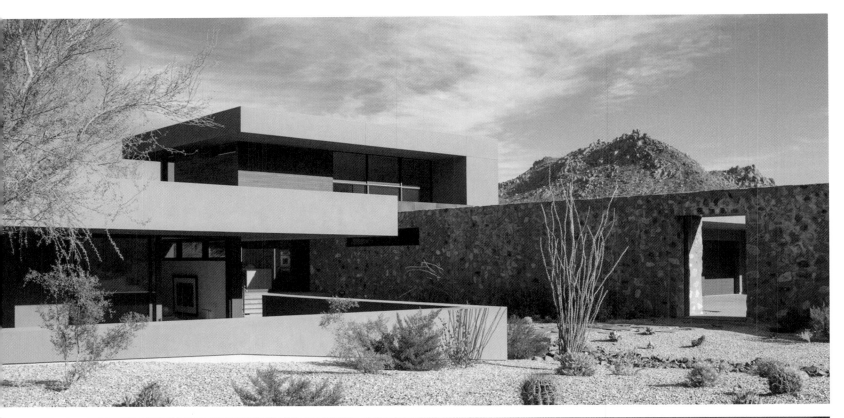

Landscape design: Marmol Radziner

Location: Scottsdale, AZ, USA
Completion: 2013
Size: 8,600 m²

Scottsdale Residence

This project blends in with the surrounding desert-like landscape. The landscape design as well as the architecture of the actual building were created in a matching union of color and design.

The Scottsdale Residence is located in a low-density development north of Scottsdale, Arizona, between Pinnacle Peak Park and the McDowell Sonoran Preserve. Through the efforts of local residents, land that was once at risk for encroaching commercial development was converted to a combination of parkland and low-density housing. The site, with habitat for Sonoran plants and wildlife, as well as the now-preserved uninhibited views of the desert landscape, called for a visually and ecologically integrated home design. The design introduced separate terraced architectural volumes connected by a bridge, allowing existing mature trees and ephemeral streams to remain in place. Local stone used on the house façade and site walls allows the structure to recede into the horizon, while subtle plantings of desert shrubs and wildflowers integrate it seamlessly into the surrounding desert landscape.

Landscape design: Landschaftsarchitektur und Umweltplanung Gerhard Kohl

Location: Leinefelde-Worbis, Germany
Completion: 2020
Size: 2,200 m²

Japanese Garden

Structured by two natural stone walls, three levels are formed, connected by a curved path. The path, paved with natural stones, leads the visitor past large boulders and appealing plantings through a Japanese archway up to the water source. This springs from an individually crafted spring stone and flows over a waterfall back down into a small pond. The curved forms, in combination with the choice of materials, convey calm and balance in the style of the Zen garden. This is underpinned by the traditional Japanese tea house, the adjoining tea garden and various other details that reveal themselves as you stroll through the garden. The interplay of rippling water, magnificent plantings and traditional elements of Japanese garden art create a retreat that brings a piece of Japan home.

The house garden combines a complex elevation situation with the flair of a Japanese garden.

Landscape design: 3SK Stylianidis Architects

Location: Heraklion, Crete, Greece
Completion: 2018
Size: 200 m²

Private Residence Heraklion

The courtyard protects the interiors from the hot summer sun whilst creating a south wind barrier during winter.

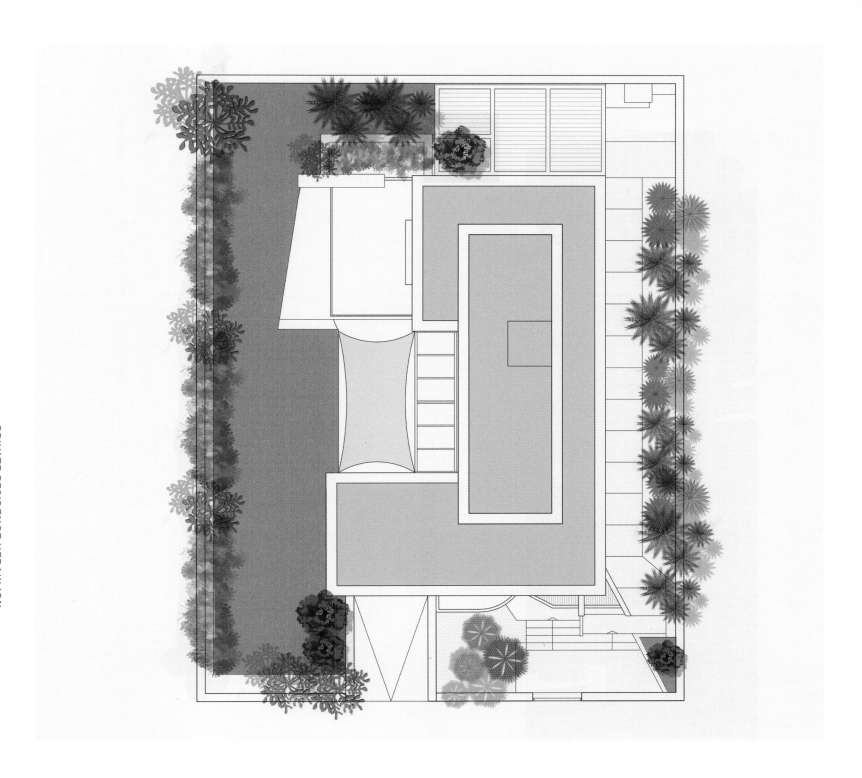

The house was designed with three wings and opens towards the north. One main feature is the paved courtyard covered by a triangular tilted sail tent surrounded by living rooms. The dining room and the kitchen are turned to the south and seperated by glazed sliding doors. The atrium like courtyard plays a main role in social life where all gatherings take place. Other smaller openings, either on the east or south, allow for internal natural local climatic control. On both sides of the living room a nook was designed where two open-sided facing gas fireplaces oppose one another. When both lit, one can see the fire from almost every corner of the ground floor. This space also acts as a connecting internal space the same way the atrium-courtyard does externally. The upper level has three bedrooms with en-suite bathrooms. In the basement, there are auxiliary spaces and car parking.

Landscape design: Möhrle und Partner, Freie
Landschaftsarchitekten

Location: Pforzheim, Germany
Completion: 2015
Size: 3,900 m²

Private Garden in Pforzheim

In 2015, the renovation of a neoclassical villa from the 1920s in the greater Stuttgart area was completed. The 3,900-square-meter residence was redesigned in a stylish yet modern way and additionally enriched by a new spacious garden. Valuable 100-year-old trees such as lime and copper beech characterize the garden in the transition to the public park and form a dignified setting for the staging of the listed ensemble. The garden was designed as a terrace garden, consistently symmetrical to the building axis. Formal trees, cut according to historical model, grow close to the house, while selected free-growing trees were placed towards the park. The residents enjoy the strong landscape reference and magnificent panoramic views from the large glass windows of the main living spaces. All walls and stone surfaces were designed from the same shell limestone, ranging from quarry-rough to polished finish. The saltwater pool enables sporty swimming. Of course a very special tree house for the children should not be missing.

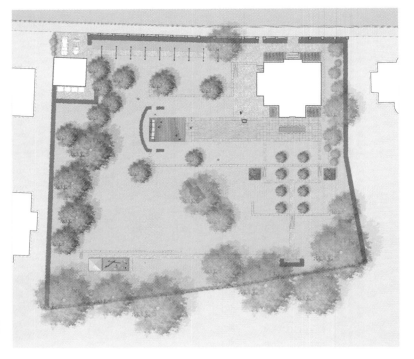

The terrace garden's transition to
the public park is characterized
by valuable 100-year-old trees.

Landscape design: SQLA Landscape
Architecture Design Studio

Location: Los Angeles, CA, USA
Completion: 2016
Size: 794 m^2

1100 Kenter

For the 1100 Kenter Ave. project an infinity pool and spa was installed. Along the edge of the pool water cascades down doubling as a simple water fountain when the pool is not in use. Right in the center of the deck is placed a simple but elegant rectangular fire-pit. Around the fire-pit a unique patchwork floor was created by installing patterned concrete on one side and staggering solid-colored rectangular concrete pavers on the other side. For further interest and texture, carpet moss was planted in the open spaces between the staggered slabs of dark grey concrete. Around the pool deck a custom wood fence was constructed that was tall enough to ensure privacy yet not tall enough to cover the picturesque canyon view outside. In accordance with the modern and minimal tastes of the homeowners, the planting palette to adorn the outer perimeter of the home consisted mainly of drought tolerate desert plants: Aloe trees, deer grass, cactus, and red yucca flowers were among some of the plants selected to display. Also on the outside a bold rocky outcrop that really made the hillside residence stand out among its neighbors. The 1100 Kenter project is an exemplary model of how minimalism can be bold and interesting without being too obvious.

For the client's affinity to entertain guests outside, a built-in BBQ and pizza oven was installed.

Landscape design: OSLO Ontwerp Stedelijke en Landschappelijke Omgeving

Location: Utrechtse Heuvelrug, The Netherlands
Completion: 2014
Size: 6,000 m²

Woodland Garden

In contrast to the straight lines of the villa, the garden has round shapes, inspired by the work of Roberto Burle Marx.

On a plot of 6,000 square meters with a height difference of six meters a villa was designed which is pushed into a dune. At the front, the dune-villa embraces a court-like space. Here the garden was designed with flowery planting areas and a long water feature. On the street side, the garden is more natural with denser planting and large birch trees. The back of the villa is directly adjacent to the existing pine forest, part of which is designed as a sloping, dense lawn. A stack of wood at the end forms the boundary of the garden. The pavement consists of 600 square meters, using the same sand-colored concrete that has also been used in the villa. The round shapes, with foothills in successive materials – concrete, semi-paved, grass – connect the courtyard with the forest.

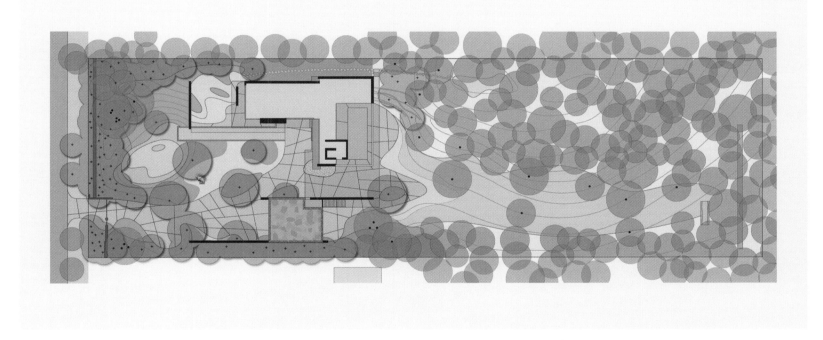

Landscape design: Horeis + Blatt
Garten- und Landschaftsarchitekten

Location: Northern Germany
Completion: 2012
Size: 6,500 m²

Garden in Northern Germany

The existing woodland scenery is used to give the garden a park-like feeling.

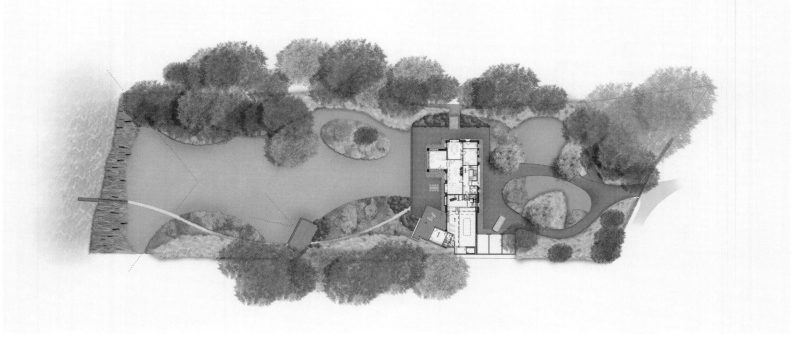

With the approach of a soft, flowing and undulating design language, the garden takes up the dynamics of the bordering water. The curved path flowing through perennial beds, in the colors of white, blue and violet, to a long pier that is leading out onto the lake. Thoughtfully planned open spaces in the garden, allow a view to the house and to the lake and also borrow a view through the neighboring gardens. In the garden large groups of boxwoods are planted in the shape of waves and spheres, as if they were coral reefs in the sea. These groups of plants on the one side provide screening and give some privacy in the garden and on the other side give a green impact to the flowerbeds in the winter months. From the eastern part of the garden – when the dining table is used in the house – there is a visual axis to the neighboring forest and to the neighboring restaurant "Fährkrug". Here, a larger group of boxwoods planted in a wavelike arrangement can be found.

Landscape design: DWY Landscape Architects
Architect: Leader Design Studio

Location: Sarasota, FL, USA
Completion: 2018
Size: 1,520 m²

Citrus Avenue

Located just south of downtown, this new home was inspired by – and grounded in – the modernist tenets of the famous Sarasota School of Architecture. With its use of open floor plans and large panes of glass, the residence manifests a clear geometry floating above the Florida landscape. It seamlessly melds architecture with the environment and provides a natural oasis in a downtown neighborhood due to the uninterrupted connection to the environment and daylight. At the heart of the site is the courtyard, where a covered porch steps down into the pool garden. The long southern exposure of the courtyard is densely planted to mask sight lines from large multistory houses across the street, and a vibrant Barragán-esque accent wall with a scupper spillway circulates water to muffle the road noise.

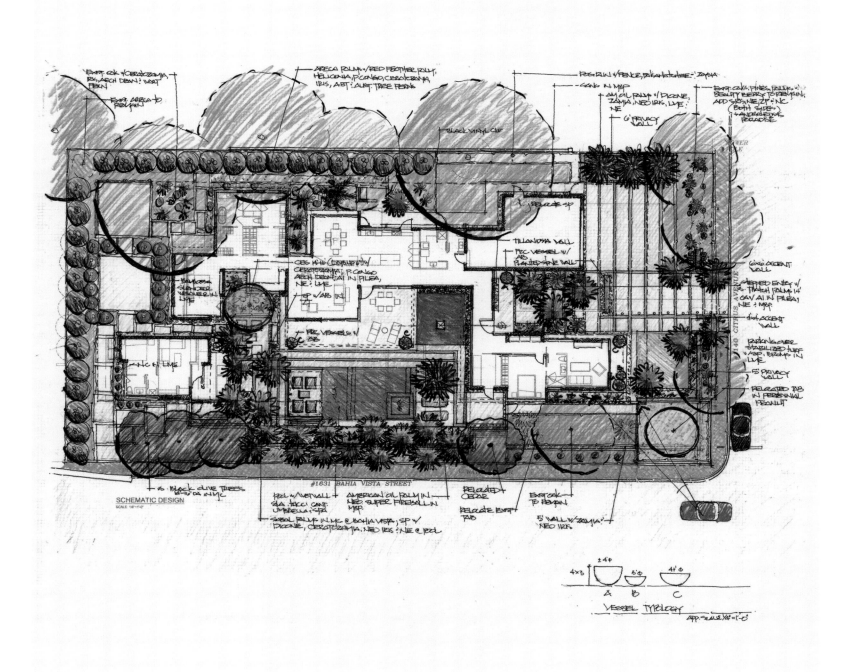

SCHEMATIC DESIGN
SCALE 1/8"=1'-0"

VESSEL TYPOLOGY
APP. SCALE 1/4"=1'-0"

Citrus Avenue creates an
oasis within an urban setting
downtown, and facilitates
an active lifestyle in this
neighborhood.

Landscape design: Horeis + Blatt
Garten- und Landschaftsarchitekten

Location: Northern Germany
Completion: 2014
Size: 900 m²

Architectural Garden

Two water basins and a water feature consisting of three natural stone objects are the highlight of the garden.

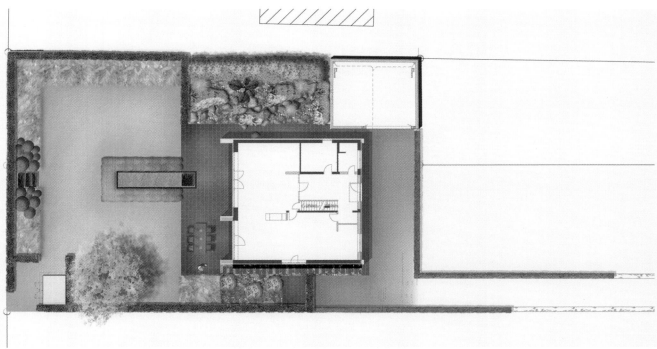

The private garden is located in a residential area characterized by villas and single-family houses and is directly adjacent to an inner-city golf course. The garden frames the centrally located residential building and is divided into different areas. In addition to the northern forecourt, small stone ridges were laid out on the long sides of the building in the western and eastern cardinal directions. The used slate stone in interaction with the selectively arranged boulders creates a design contrast to the selective plantings of grasses and a bonsai. The eastern rock garden also has a breakfast terrace with a direct connection to the kitchen of the house, where the first rays of sunshine of the day can be enjoyed. Large-format slabs of Swedish granite lead on both sides of the building to the southern area of the property, the garden proper. In front of the house there is a large terrace area. The terrace represents an extension of the adjacent living space and at the same time it functions as the starting point of the water axis running centrally through the garden.

Landscape design: Marmol Radziner

Location: Montecito, CA, USA
Completion: 2011
Size: 4,900 m²

Lilac Drive Residence

Old-growth and sensitively added trees complement each other in this gentle topography.

The Lilac Drive Residence is situated at the base of the Romero Canyon Trailhead, between the town of Montecito to the south and the Santa Ynez Mountains to the north. The site's ample sunlight, gentle topography, groves of old-growth trees, and natural stream, together encapsulate the character of the surrounding region which the clients had fallen captive to during annual visits. They envisioned a new vacation home that would preserve the site's character, bring the outdoors in, and maximize the opportunities for outdoor living. The architects and landscape architects of Marmol Radziner worked collaboratively to integrate the new structure into the site. Careful planning resulted in a terraced home with garden spaces that preserve the site's subtle slope and mature trees, and green roofs and permeable materials that maintain existing hydrological patterns. Throughout the construction process, the design-build approach allowed for adaptability on a complex and sensitive site.

Landscape design: auböck+karasz landscape architects, Vienna

Location: Correns, Provence, France
Completion: 2019
Size: 16,500 m²

Villa Mont Doux

A hortus conclusus of open spaces: spacious terraces, quiet places for reflection, a pétanque court in the shade next to white flowering oleander and roses.

A hamlet of gardens and houses lies on the outskirts of Correns. This rough wild place of pines and holm oaks has been gradually tamed inwards – towards living. A garden of open spaces between the buildings was created. The hillside location promises exact western exposure with views over forests and hills. The materials and design language in the tradition of Provence were interpreted by Architect Weichenberger in a contemporary way with the use of natural stone, local tiles and terracotta pots. The framed view stages the diversity of the surroundings like a stage set. The passage of the sun through the seasons determines the treatment of light and shadow. The loft, as the central living area, opens glassily into the courtyard, with a view to the sleeping house "Ciel" towards the Montagne Sainte-Victoire. Next to it is the studio, a cube generated from the form of the hamlet, private and integrated. Strips of rosemary and lavender frame these buildings, and below the dwelling house the old stone terraces have been supplemented and planted with apricots and young olive trees.

Landscape design: Guz Architects

Location: Singapore
Completion: 2018
Size: 2,000 m²

Olive House

The Olive House has a site area of 2,000 square meters where one can find a large plot of land with beautiful mature trees around its perimeter. As the road is lowered on one side of the house, it is being used for a "basement" entry where the garage and all service spaces could be located without using the valuable ground floor level. So it was possible to maximize the garden areas. In order to fulfill the desire of the nature-loving client, the house is made up of pavilions separated by cooling water courtyards. This allows for maximum cooling airflow in Singapore's hot humid tropical climate. Concrete was only used where necessary for basements and floor slabs. Steel with its lighter carbon footprint was used for columns above ground and roof structure. The aluminum roof was also heavily insulated to reduce solar gain before being topped off with a large array of photovoltaic cells.

Outward views of the site are limited; therefore an internal courtyard is introduced to give interesting inward views.

Landscape design: doxiadis+
Architects & Landscape Architects

Location: Antiparos Island, Greece
Completion: ongoing
Size: 350,000 m^2

Landscapes of Cohabitation

After thousands of years of existence, the beautiful Greek landscapes now face extensive transformations. This project attempts to reverse the trend of transformation as destruction by strategizing transformation as a new synthesis, a cohabitation. The strategy developed is reading and extrapolating the site's existing elements, to create a skeleton for all new ones. While normally roads zig-zag down hillsides causing more destruction than the houses themselves, here they are either perpendicular to the hillside or parallel. The second layer is vegetation dynamics. Closer to the houses the plants are placed at greater densities and provide for a tended garden. As distances from the house increase density diminishes, providing space for natural re-vegetation between the placed plants. Beyond a certain distance from the house no plants are placed, allowing for completely natural re-vegetation. So, a gradient is formed from the tended garden to native nature, synthesizing the two into a new cohabitation.

New strategies to demonstrate
how to construct on beautiful
Cycladic landscapes without de-
stroying them.

Landscape design: heri&salli

Location: Upper Austria
Completion: 2013
Size: 500 m²

Landscape Fence

Architecture in this case is
an accumulation of possibilities
within a circumscribed space and
forms only the edges for a wide
land in between.

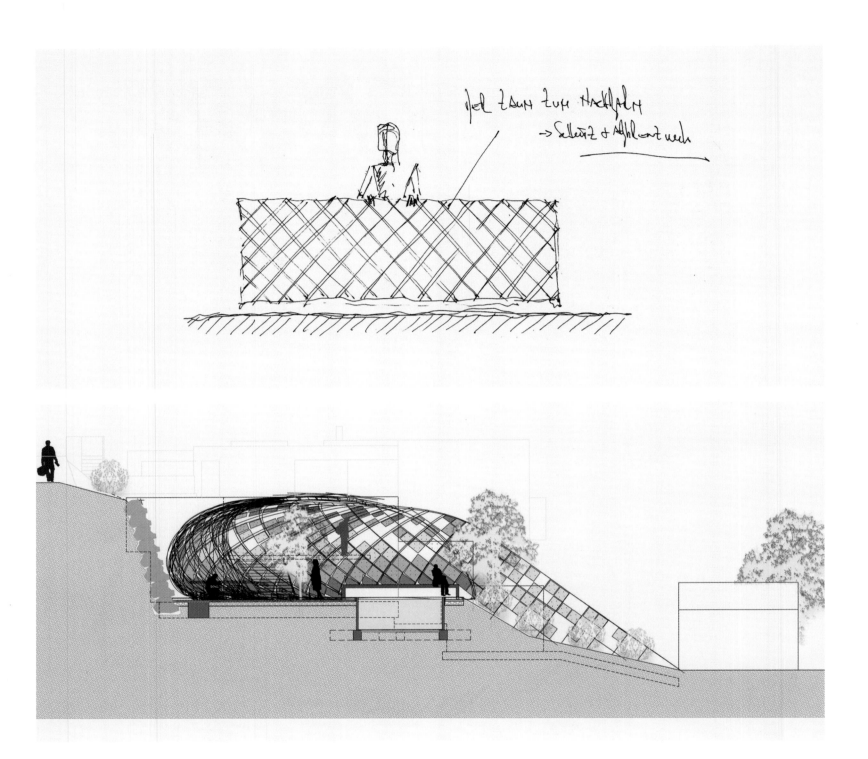

In the garden of a private builder in Austria, a cocoon-like steel framework was built around a swimming pool. With suspended panels and more or less function-dependent fixtures, the parametrically organized spatial structure circumscribes possibilities of usable and experienceable surfaces. Based on the task of redesigning an existing garden plot with a lake view and at the same time creating a visual screen and a boundary towards surrounding properties and neighbors, the theme of a classic hunter's fence was taken up. A fence functions as a protection or boundary. In a broader sense, it also serves as an aesthetic element or representative sign. It does not demarcate space, but forms it and makes it experienceable. The aim of the opening cocoon-like structure is to create different local qualities and experiential spaces. Partly covered, withdrawn and protected, then opening and in between or to finally float out of it in the water of the pool.

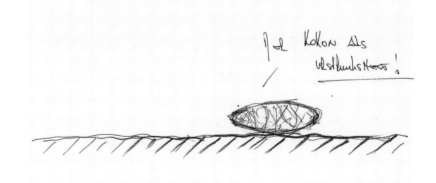

Landscape design: Floor Associates

Location: Paradise Valley, AZ, USA
Completion: 2016
Size: 4,455 m^2

Nita Residence

Surrounded by salvaged ironwoods, Foothill Palo Verdes, succulents and cacti, Nita Residence extends over 4,000 square meters.

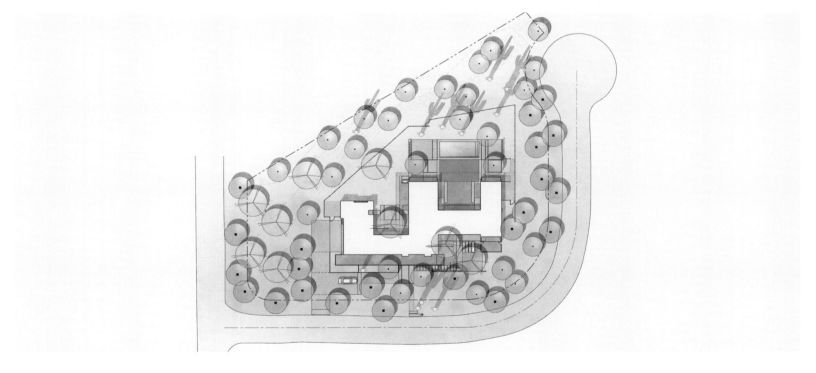

The Nita Residence is located in Arizona's Paradise Valley and blends in with the surrounding desert-like landscape. Designed to blur the lines between the indoor and outdoor spaces, this private residence celebrates the Sonoran Desert and all its flora. The design introduces a series of distinctive courtyards that pull the residents from within the glass interior to an exterior composition of color, texture, and pattern in the immersive desert landscape. Each courtyard is unique and includes such features as an outdoor shower at the master bath, a minimalist water feature at the main entry, integrated seatwalls and a linear fire feature. Specimen trees, such as large salvaged ironwoods and Foothill Palo Verdes, provide filtered shade for the owners' dramatic collection of succulents and cacti.

Architecture: Durbach Block Jaggers Architects
Landscape design: Myles Baldwin Design and
Bates Landscape

Location: Point Piper, Australia
Completion: 2020
Size: 250 m²

House Taurus

The site is directly adjacent to Sydney Harbour and a private beach. The astonishing sea level connection to the beach is bracketed by beautiful landscaping, fig trees and jetties. A fully planted roof garden adds substantial planting to this harbour edge site, creating a garden outlook for all of the neighbouring buildings and settling the seamlessly house into its site. A mature frangipani is accommodated in mounded soil. A rich mixture of ground covers, succulents and shrubs create a seasonal, scented and flowering garden. Slender character trees, Mexican Fan Palms and screw palms, occupy a grassy terrace providing fast moving shadows on the concrete façade. Mounded boundary planting of elephants ears, clivia, and monstera deliciosa combine with rich groundcover fabric of creeping fig, bleeding heart vine and bougainvillea to soften the site's edges.

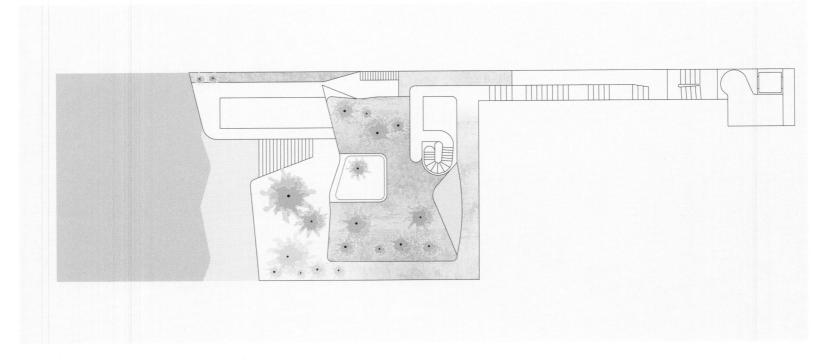

The immediacy of the water, a
vast and changing sky and the
action of a working harbor ani-
mate the rooms and gardens at
all levels.

Landscape design: Damilanostudio Architects

Location: Piemont, Italy
Completion: 2019
Size: 1,300 m²

IE Villa

The project's inspiration was affected by the hectic life that distinguishes its inhabitants, and at the same time by the feeling of serenity and calm inside temples and houses.

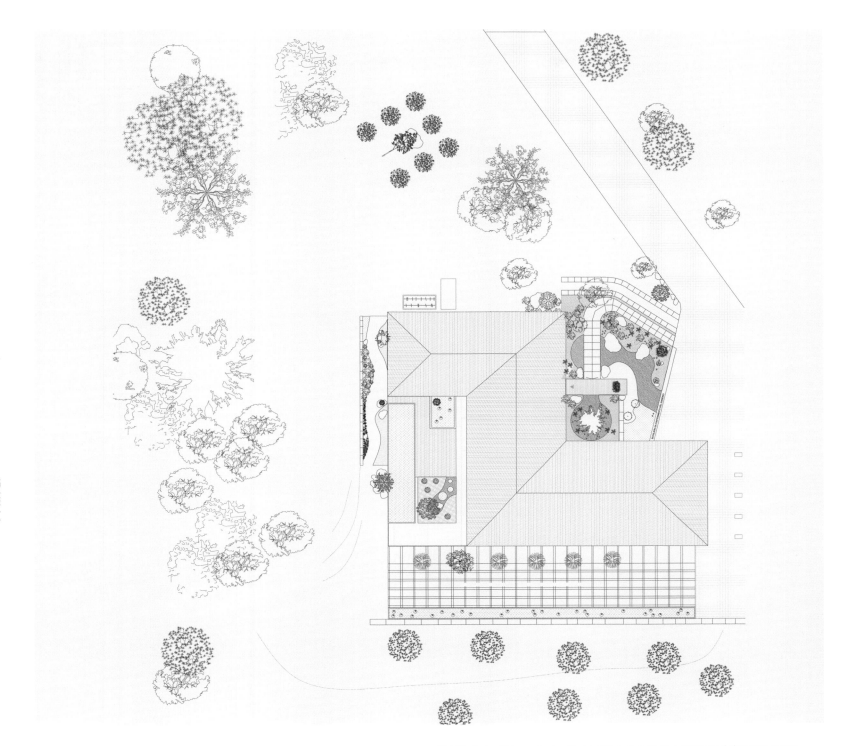

IE Villa is built in a strategic position due to the view and the exposure. The site enjoys a panoramic view of the Alpine Alps and the plain below. The entrance to the villa can be reached through a stone staircase completely merged with nature. Responsible for the realization of the garden was Roagna Vivai in Cuneo. They placed the Corallo armchair by Edra on the walkway, a place designed to relax and for contemplation toward the suggestive landscape. Through sliding windows the owner can access a charming teak terrace and a long swimming pool which benefit of an excellent southern exposure. In the garden, taken from traditional Japanese architecture, there are two large ponds: one with water and water lilies and the other one with a Japanese garden. The entire outdoor space is designed in great detail both in terms of the choice of materials and vegetation. Green areas from Japanese tradition are presented in the entrance space and along the pool area. In this space local rocks of different sizes have been re-proposed.

Landscape design: Design Workshop

Location: Aspen, CO, USA
Completion: 2013
Size: 35,000 m²

DBX Ranch

With a significant reforestation of Ponderosa pine, over 6,200 square meters of previously disturbed landscape is restored into a native meadow.

Until recently, this 14,000 square kilometers property was the maintenance boneyard for a nearby working ranch. The residence – a compound of structures designed in the modern ranch vernacular – is now unified by the careful placement of layered and interconnected outdoor gathering spaces and curated native plant communities. The owners wanted to create a family retreat that would celebrate the idea of seamless indoor-outdoor living. Located at an elevation of 2,300 meters the property commands panoramic views to the east, south and west. Although designed to accommodate large gatherings of friends and family, the courtyard maintains a sense of intimacy within the expansive environment. Resting beneath a dappled canopy of aspen trees, the family's dining table serves as a centerpiece. A stone veranda, enclosed by a low stone seating wall and shaded by a steel trellis, expands the kitchen, living, and dining rooms into the physical landscape, offering a promontory from which to view the meadow.

Landscape design:
Kumpfmüller Landschaftsarchitektur

Location: Behamberg, Austria
Completion: 2015
Size: 160 m²

Private Garden in Behamberg

Lovingly selected garden furniture and sculptures adorn the wall crowns, niches and landings.

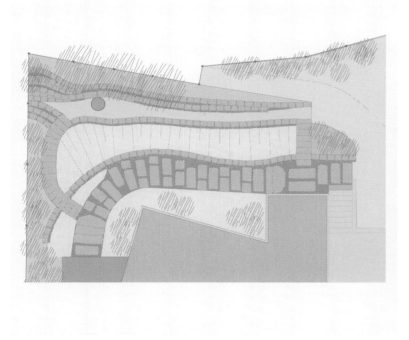

The steep south-facing bank behind the private house was wooded and run to seed. The aim was to make the area readily accessible again, including a small seating area from which a panoramic view into to the valley and its opposite side could be enjoyed. The area was split into a sequential series of terraced dry stone walls created from local limestone slabs connected together by steps, and completed with a gravel path running at right-angles to them. In the gaps between the limestone slabs, suitable wild plants were carefully placed during the wall building. The indigenous plants included pink carthusians, wild woodland strawberries and hawkweed. These wild plants will ultimately spread throughout the garden and will be greatly attractive to butterflies, bees and birds.

Kua Bay Residence

The Kua Bay Residence embeds
man-made aesthetic in two
extremes of the Hawaiian
landscape: the mountain and
the ocean.

This residence is located on Hawaii's dry, volcanic Kona shore and extends over 3,112 square meters. Its design draws on the elemental forces that shaped the land to contextualize its material design and embeds human aesthetic experience within the landscape. The site is on a transect from a mountain top to the ocean, two extremes of the Hawaiian landscape. The design teams worked closely to develop a series of indoor-outdoor living spaces that trace a narrative from the mountain to the ocean, taking cues from Hawaii's geological and cultural history. Materials were carefully chosen to serenely distill the colors and textures of this unique place.
A sequence of spaces emerges from a cleft in lava bedrock, proceeds through a freshwater oasis-like interior courtyard, finally opening out to an expansive view of the ocean. The visitor's journey terminates at the pool deck with the merging of constructed pool and ocean. The pool's far edge seems to disappear, creating a seamless connection to the vast ocean.

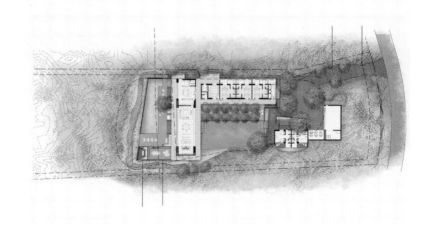

Landscape design: -GardScape- private gardens by Christoph Harreiss

Location: Zirndorf, Germany
Completion: 2012
Size: 350 m²

The Garden of Opposites

The large sunken terrace serves as a community terrace while the smaller circular sunken terrace was created to function as a retreat. Both areas were provided with a small staircase, framed with granite steles and covered with decking boards. Planting areas were then created and planted around both terraces, allowing people to experience nature up close.
To meet the desire of a low-maintenance and modern garden, the planting areas were covered with weed foil and granite gravel. This highlights the flower colors of the plants. To create a natural contrast, a stream was integrated into the planting area as a further highlight. This gives the garden a natural charm and look. The brown bamboo fence and the lawn bring calmness into the garden due to their uniformity and form the contrast to the planted stone areas. The planting is very colorful and richly flowering. In order to enjoy the garden in the evening hours and in the winter time, spotlights were installed in the planting areas in the entire garden.

The downwards shifted terraces give the garden another dimension and open up a whole new perspective of the garden to the viewer.

Landscape design: DS Architecture
Architect: NSMH Architects

Location: Sariyer, Istanbul, Turkey
Completion: 2005
Size: 2,200 m²

Özen House

With the help of mossiness due to the overflow of the pond's water, water lily pond and swimming pool are perceived as parts of habitat.

Being attached to an existing building, Özen House' new landscape design is separated with a pebble line that intensifies its state of being an add-on. The garden gained a graphic texture with different function levels as orchard, sun bathing area, swimming area, sports and parking area, seperated in horizontal directions by 20 centimeter inclines, which gives the perception of agricultural terraces. Waterlily pond and swimming pool are integrated due to the overflow of the vegetative pond's water. Both, cultivatable plantation and the selected Bosphorus plantation support the existing local orchard culture and the existing ecosystem. This garden concept was integrated into the environment with a framework made of metal, which does not conceal the graphic texture from outsiders' views. Functioning as a door to the parking area, this "metal wall" also forms the façade of the garden. It behaves like the continuation of the street with its semi-transparency and was designed to always show its metal bars as well as its green texture.

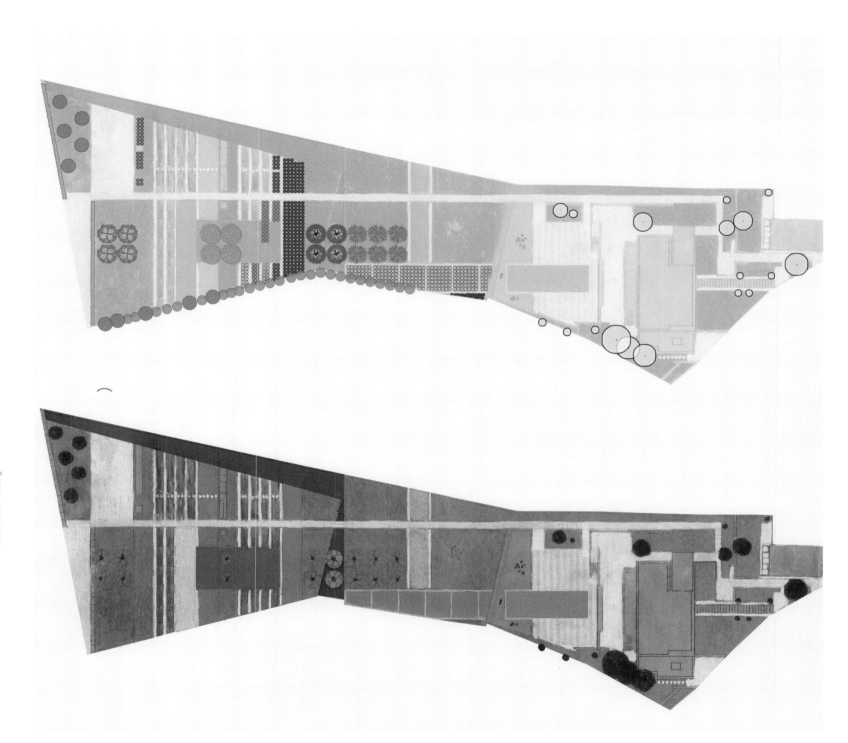

Landscape design: MDL

Location: Esch-sur-Alzette, Luxembourg
Completion: 2012
Size: 90 m^2

Terrace Garden

This project was created between the façades and walls of the client's house. The wooden terrace opens up a magnificent view on the different parts of the court that are planted with perennials, grasses and trees. The plants seem to grow out of the wood panels of the terrace floor which underlines a connection to nature. Through the open design of the terrace, a central meeting point for the inhabitants was created. A water basin makes out a highlight of the garden. Its sounds of flowing water create a relaxing audible. All in all, this terrace offers retreat and invites to linger.

This garden mainly consists of a wooden floor, creating a light-filled terrace. It is open to the surroundings but at the same time shielded by walls creating privacy.

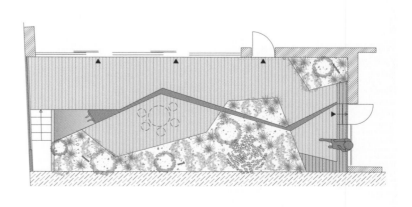

Landscape design: Grupo de Diseño Urbano
Architecture: Carranza and Ruiz Arquitectura

Location: Saltillo, Coahuila, Mexico
Completion: 2018
Size: 7,832 m²

La Casa de los Muros

With a site area of 11,000 square meters, this residence gyrates around gardens, a central plaza, a large interior courtyard and diverse intimate gardens. The architectural and landscape architectural project was designed for a young Mexican family. It is a project that highlights scale in interior and exterior spaces, seeking to correctly meet the interests and needs of its inhabitants and trying to generate the home that despite being large in its spaces has that magic that only proportion and scale can achieve. It was developed almost entirely on a single floor, taking advantage of the generous site and topographical flatness. The design is based on two large squares, the first one with an orthogonal plan, a large water mirror and and the massive marble wall that creates the access, the second one with a combination of stone pavement and magnificient oak trees embraces part of the social spaces of the house: kitchen and dining, living room, outdoor bar and interior swimming pool, with an exterior fireplace and lounge area. Other intimate gardens are connected to the master suite and childrens' bedrooms.

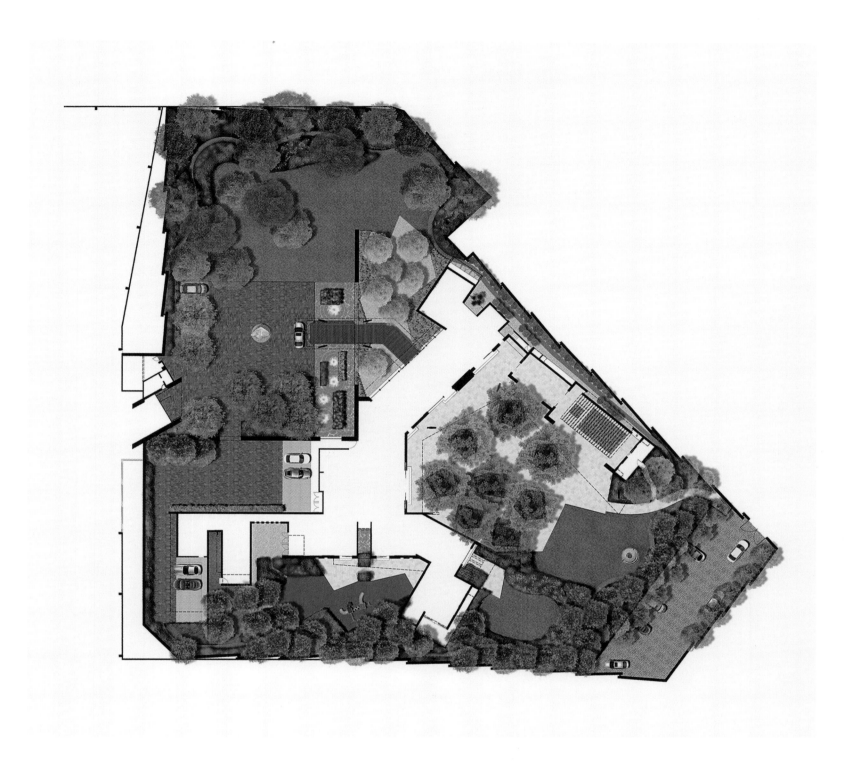

This residence gyrates around gardens, a central plaza, a large interior courtyard and diverse intimate gardens.

Landscape design: GTL Michael Triebswetter
Landschaftsarchitekt

Location: Kaliningrad, Russia
Completion: 2014
Size: 690 m²

Private Garden Kaliningrad

Inside and outside, shell limestone was chosen as the
consistent material for walls,
flooring and outdoor terraces.

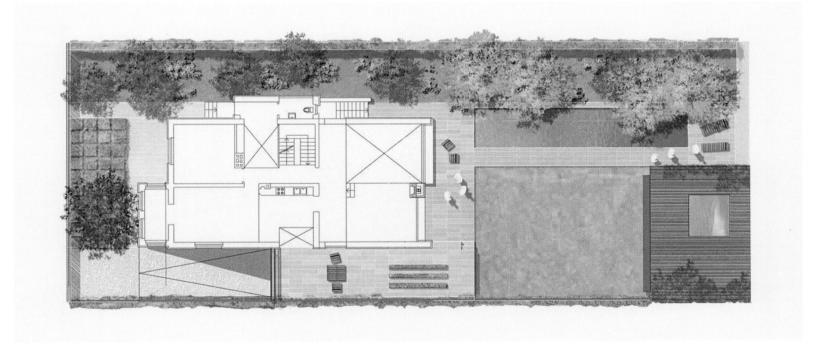

In a typical 1920s housing estate suburb, a garden paradise was created which is barely perceptible from the street side. The original house, restored with great attention to detail, was extended into the depths of the garden by a residential hall of identical cubature to the original building and connected via a glass joint. A clear geometric framework organizes the garden into spaces of completely different character. The grove of Japanese cherries, underplanted with perennials, hydrangeas and rhododendrons not only screens the neighboring buildings, but is also a romantic retreat on hot summer days. Attached to it, the water lily pool creates a generous distance between the sauna house and the residential hall as well as between the cherry grove and the lawn. The pool is supplied with fresh water via a high water wall at the boundary of the property. The sauna house is placed between the water wall and a second, rose-covered wall slice in such a way as to create an additional sheltered seating area that is only partially visible from the main house.

Landscape design: Terragram

Location: Sydney, Australia
Completion: 2011
Size: 430 m²

An Edible Garden

This garden is one of the first in Sydney's upmarket suburb that combines the aesthetic aspects of a garden with the production of own food. It is an indication of an ever-increasing awareness related to the origin of the food. Sydney's climate is suitable for a wide range of subtropical fruit and vegetables. The edible plants are also used for privacy. Olive trees, passionfruit on fences, lemon hedges and bamboo perform a role normally assigned to purely decorative plants. The garden initially incorporated a small area of lawn for ball games which now assumes a more decorative role. The entry court is more traditional and acts as a social place. Tall retaining walls contain numerous niches for sitting and horizontal resting. A shallow wading pool escaped draconian Australian rules that require fencing off any water deeper than 300 milimeters. This explains the stainless steel palisade fence. Also, the client decided to beautify and pave a narrow lane. A preferred one color of Gazania transformed bloom in a color orgy, much admired by passers-by.

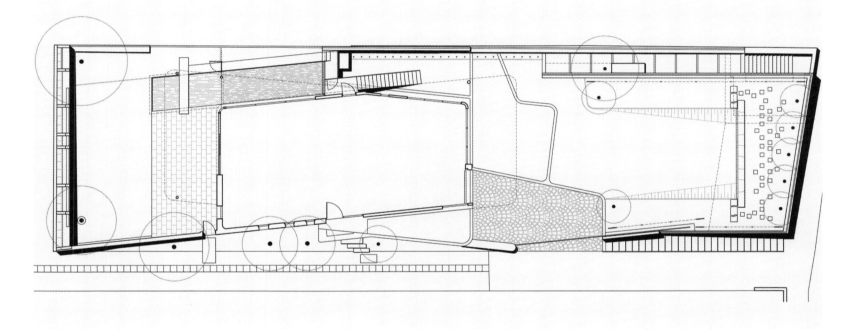

It is not a garden where green fingers of owners are not desirable, just the opposite. It requires owners to clip, fertilize and also eat this garden.

Landscape design: Topiaris Landscape Architecture

Location: Comporta, Portugal
Completion: 2010
Size: 3,000 m²

Garden in Comporta

Located in Herdade da Comporta, on the southwest coast of Portugal, this garden blends in an outstanding and diverse landscape mosaic. Its high ecological and cultural value, with psammophilous pioneer vegetation, and maritime and umbrella pines on Holocene dunes, is complemented by vast extensions of farmland and rice fields on the lower alluvial soils. The plot and its boundaries merge with this scenario, although surrounded by several road paths. The design was inspired by the surrounding landscape, creating a specific aesthetics that is rooted in the ecological characteristics of the region. Planting of native species was carried out in clusters with mounds that gradually expanded to adjacent areas, fostering natural progression, translated into changeable and transitory scenarios. Visual privacy, a small water tank and cool shades were considered and integrated into the design. A drip irrigation system supported the initial phases of the vegetation, but was disabled, as the natural regeneration took its place.

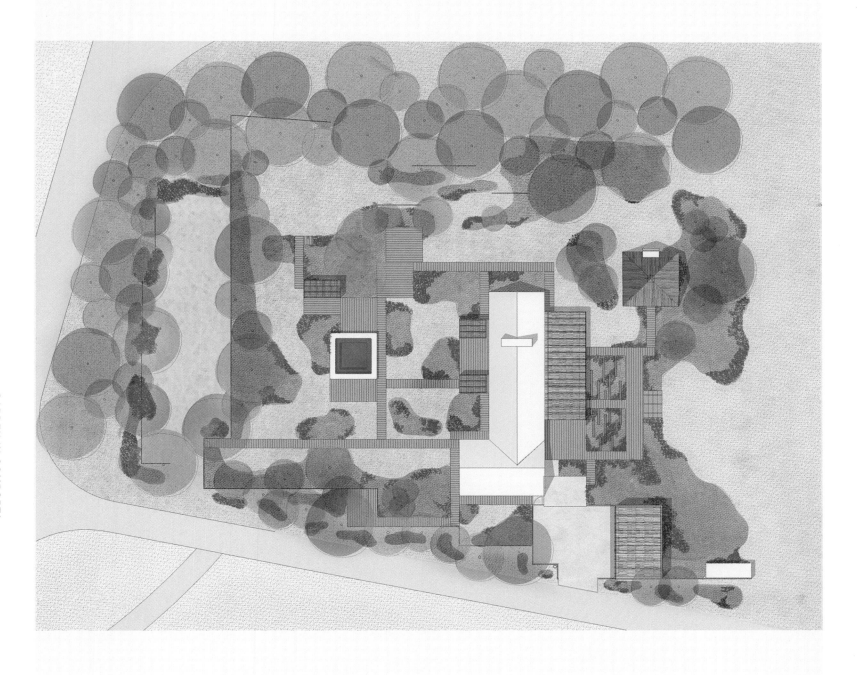

The main structure is defined by wood walkways with orthogonal lines, slightly raised from the soil to protect the planted native vegetation from trampling.

Landscape design and architect: Alexander
Brenner Architekten

Location: Stuttgart, Deutschland
Completion: 2019
Size: 500 m^2

Brenner Research House PR39

The green garden at the house blends gently into the hillside of Stuttgart.

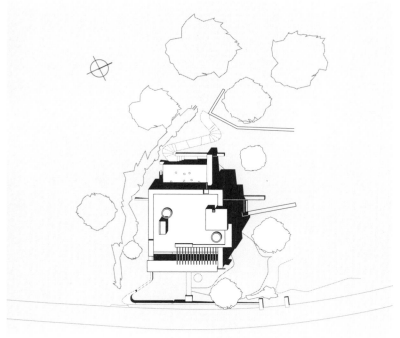

The Brenner Research House, located on a steep slope in the north of Stuttgart, is surrounded by a gently undulating, flowing garden that overlays the steepness and continues above the base structure with the garages to the street. The multifaceted, flowing forms are created by wave-cut planting groups. In the eastern part, solid walls encroach on the undulating landscape from the house. This creates an exciting contrast between the built and the gentle sweep of the green. The house also rises castle-like cubic from the soft womb of nature. The buildings and the landscaping have a completely different language of form and thus each stands confidently and uniquely for itself. The difference is celebrated and respected. Landscape remains landscape and house remains house and so they enhance each other.

Landscape design: Leon Kluge Design

Location: Chushi Village, Chang'an Town, China
Completion: 2021
Size: 800 m²

African Heartbeat

It is the crooked wood that is the best sculpture.

The African Heartbeat is a garden that invites you to experience the unique sensation of African hospitality. Being surrounded by natural elements such as grass, wood, and water, one feels at peace with only natural elements coming together to wrap its arms around you. Africa's flair for celebration comes to life in the decorative paintwork which depicts the diversity of life on the African plains. Water is the energy that connects the natural elements and allows a sense of peace and contemplation throughout the garden. The sound of water falling adds to the wildness and reminds one of a peaceful African escape. Taking inspiration from the African savanna, grasses become the most important feature. They too – like the water – flow and move according to natures gentle forces. In a world where it is easy to lose our connection with nature, the sound of the heartbeat of Africa easily pulls us together with the power of love.

Landscape design: Floor Associates

Location: Paradise Valley, AZ, USA
Completion: 2010
Size: 3,035 m²

Paradise Valley Residence

The design's sculptural forms and seasonal color energize the landscape while complementing the architecture.

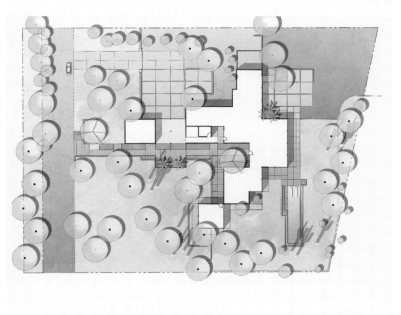

The Paradise Valley Residence, a renovation of a classic 1950s mid-century modern residence located in Paradise Valley, Arizona. The major components of the design included the careful integration of a negative-edge infinity pool, oriented on Camelback Mountain. In total, Paradise Valley Residence extends to over 3,000 square meters. The landscape's existing palette was updated and complemented by the addition of new specimens emphasizing sculptural forms and seasonal color intended to energize the landscape while complementing the architecture and new hardscape design. The project has been widely recognized as a prime example of the blending of modern architecture and modern landscape architecture into a beautiful expression of desert living.

Index A–Z

Image Directory

Imprint

ISBN 978-3-03768-269-2
© 2022 by Braun Publishing AG
www.braun-publishing.ch

1st edition 2022

Editor: Editorial Office van Uffelen
Editorial staff and layout: Carola Moser,
Maikhoi Tran, Lara Wörner
Graphic concept: Martin Denker,
KOSMOS – Visuelle Kommunikation, Münster
Reproduction: Bild1 Druck GmbH, Berlin

Cover front (from left to right, from above
to below): Bill Timmerman, Gürkan Akay,
Christiaan de Bruijne, Greg Wilson
Cover back: Die Schmiede